The Science of Living Things

What are Food Chains and Webs?

Bobbie Kalman & Jacqueline Langille

Crabtree Publishing Company

The Science of Living Things Series
A Bobbie Kalman Book

**For April and Ron Fast
and Luke the GO GO machine**

Editor-in-Chief
Bobbie Kalman

Writing team
Bobbie Kalman
Jacqueline Langille

Managing editor
Lynda Hale

Editors
Greg Nickles
April Fast

Text and photo research
Jacqueline Langille
Tara Harte

Computer design
Lynda Hale
McVanel Communications Inc.
(cover concept)

Production coordinator
Hannelore Sotzek

Consultant
K. Diane Eaton, Hon. B.Sc., B.A.,
Brock University

Photographs
Photo Researchers, Inc.: E.R. Degginger: page 15 (bottom left)
   Tom McHugh/Steinhart Aquarium: page 14
   Dr. Paul A. Zahl: page 11 (bottom)
Tom Stack & Associates: Perry Conway: pages 28-29
   David M. Dennis: pages 20 (bottom), 21 (top)
   Jeff Foott: page 21 (bottom)
   Mark Newman: page 18
Other photographs by Digital Vision and Digital Stock

Illustrations
Barbara Bedell: pages 4, 9, 10, 22-23, 24-25, 30
Halina Below-Spada: pages 26-27

Printer
Worzalla Publishing Company

Color separations and film
Dot 'n Line Image Inc.

Crabtree Publishing Company

PMB 16A
350 Fifth Avenue
Suite 3308
New York
N.Y. 10118

612 Welland Avenue
St. Catharines
Ontario, Canada
L2M 5V6

73 Lime Walk
Headington
Oxford OX3 7AD
United Kingdom

Cataloging in Publication Data
Kalman, Bobbie
   What are food chains and webs?

(The science of living things)
Includes index.

ISBN 0-86505-876-8 (library bound)   ISBN 0-86505-888-1 (pbk.)
This book introduces food chains and webs, featuring both herbivores
and carnivores. Energy, food production, and decomposition in various
ecosystems are also discussed.

1. Food chains (Ecology)—Juvenile literature. [1. Food chains (Ecology)
2. Ecology] I. Title. II. Series: Kalman, Bobbie. Science of living things.

QH541.14.K3497 1998   j577'.16   LC 98-14714
                                                    CIP

Contents

What is a food chain?

*A food chain includes plants, a plant-eating animal called a **herbivore**, a meat-eating animal called a **carnivore**, an animal that eats dead animal bodies called a **scavenger**, and tiny creatures, or **decomposers**, that break down dead plant or animal remains.*

All animals eat other living things. Some animals eat plants. Others feed on the plant-eaters. For example, lettuce is eaten by a rabbit, which is eaten by a wolf. This pattern of eating and being eaten is called a **food chain**. There are countless food chains, and every plant and animal belongs to at least one.

herbivore

carnivore

scavenger

decomposers

Food chains connect

When an animal from one food chain eats a member of another food chain, two food chains connect. The diagram on the right shows two food chains connecting. The chipmunk and the mouse eat both nuts and berries. The mink and the owl might eat a chipmunk one day and a mouse the next. When food chains connect, the pattern is called a **food web**. Food webs usually include many plants and animals.

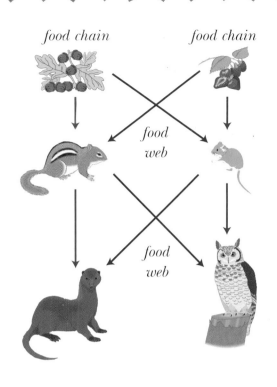

food chain   *food chain*

food web

food web

Food webs and ecosystems

Each **ecosystem** on earth contains many food chains. An ecosystem includes all the plants, animals, and non-living natural things, such as sand, rocks, and soil, in a certain area. Deserts, forests, coral reefs in the ocean, and African grasslands called **savannahs** are examples of different ecosystems. All the living things in an ecosystem are connected in a food web, and they depend on one another for survival.

In one African savannah food chain, springboks eat the grass, and the lion hunts springboks for food.

Energy from food

Every living thing needs food in order to live. Food provides the **nutrients** plants and animals need to build and repair parts of their body. Food also provides **energy**, or power. Without energy, plants cannot grow. Animals also use energy to grow, breathe, move, and do the things that allow them to survive. Think of ten ways you use energy every day.

Almost all the energy on earth comes from sunlight. Green plants trap some of the sun's energy to turn it into food. They are the only living things that can make their own food using sunlight. When an animal eats a plant, the stored energy from the sunlight is passed on to that animal. The energy is passed along the food chain once more when another animal eats the first animal.

Energy lost along the way

There is a large amount of energy at the beginning of every food web, but much of it is lost as it passes from one living thing to another. A herbivore's body **absorbs**, or takes in, only a small amount of the energy stored in the plants it eats. A carnivore then absorbs a small amount of the energy in a herbivore's body.

Fewer living things

The diagram below shows the levels of a food web. There are many plants on the first level because sunlight provides the energy plants need to survive. Fewer herbivores can survive than plants because energy is lost as it is passed along the food web. At the top of the pyramid, there is only enough energy to keep a few carnivores alive.

Energy pyramid

*This diagram shows that because of energy lost, there are fewer living things at each level of a food web. It is called an **energy pyramid** because it is wide at the bottom and narrow at the top.*

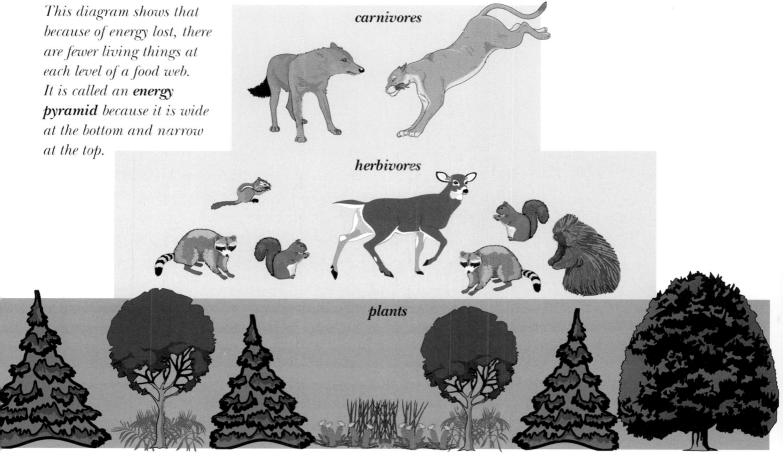

carnivores

herbivores

plants

Plants are producers

Plants make up the first level of all food chains and webs in the world. Green plants are called **primary producers**, or the first food-makers in a food chain or web. They make all the food energy found in an ecosystem. People and other living things could not survive without the food energy made by plants.

Using light to make food

Plants use sunlight to make food. They use the sun's energy to make different types of sugar. Using the energy from sunlight, they combine water with **carbon dioxide**, a gas found in the air. This food-making process is called **photosynthesis**. When a plant needs energy to grow, it uses up some of the sugar to feed itself.

What photosynthesis needs

For photosynthesis to occur, plants use more than just sunlight. They use a green substance found in their leaves, called **chlorophyll**. Chlorophyll catches the energy from sunlight. Plants take carbon dioxide from the air through their leaves and absorb water and nutrients from the soil through their roots.

Trees, grasses, herbs, and vines are green plants. All green plants use photosynthesis to make food. The word photosynthesis means "putting together with light." Photosynthesis usually happens in a plant's leaves.

The air we breathe

Food is an important product of photosynthesis, but photosynthesis also makes large amounts of **oxygen**, a gas in the air. Animals need oxygen to survive. Without plants, the earth's air would soon run out of oxygen and people and animals would die.

During photosynthesis, plants also take large amounts of carbon dioxide from the air. Even though this gas is a natural part of air, it can be harmful. Too much carbon dioxide could make the earth heat up more than normal and harm most living things.

Photosynthesis

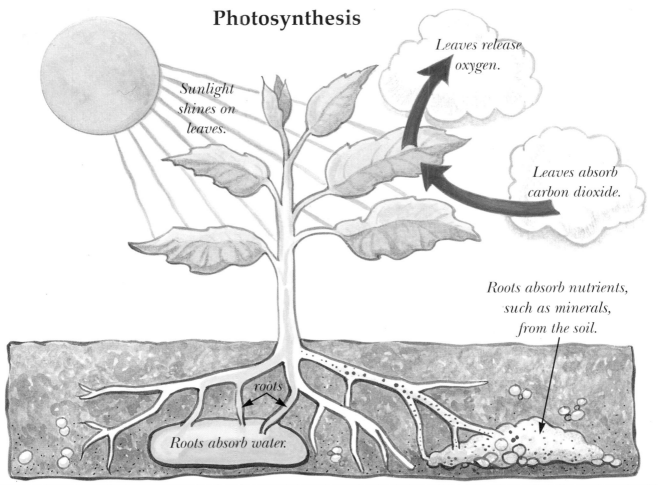

Sunlight shines on leaves.

Leaves release oxygen.

Leaves absorb carbon dioxide.

Roots absorb nutrients, such as minerals, from the soil.

roots

Roots absorb water.

Water Plants

Plants are an important part of water ecosystems. A water food chain starts with tiny floating plants called **phytoplankton**. They change the sun's energy into food, just as plants do on land. They also provide fish with the oxygen they need in order to survive underwater.

Seaweeds such as kelp are the largest ocean plants. They belong to the **algae family** along with phytoplankton. They have a plant body but no roots, stem, or leaves. They only grow in shallow water, where sunlight can reach them.

Sunlight does not go very deep into water, so seaweed only grows at the surface or in shallow water.

Tiny producers

Phytoplankton, which are also called algae, are so small that scientists need **microscopes** to study them. Phytoplankton are called plants, but they have no roots, stems, or leaves. They live in almost every water ecosystem in the world, including ponds, lakes, marshes, and oceans. They float near the surface of the water because they need sunlight to make food and oxygen. The oxygen they make goes into the water and air. Ocean algae make more than half of the earth's oxygen!

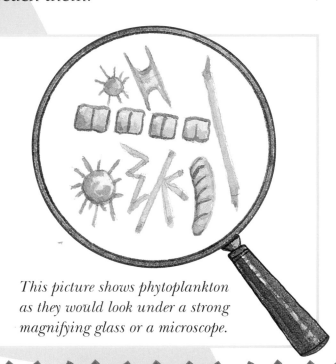

This picture shows phytoplankton as they would look under a strong magnifying glass or a microscope.

Desert plants

In some ecosystems, animals must eat plants to get water as well as food. Deserts are ecosystems that receive very little rain. Desert plants, especially cacti, are good at storing water. The stems have a waxy covering to keep water from leaving the plant. Spines on the stem protect the plants from being eaten. In order to get at stored water, some animals have a special mouth that can bore into desert plants. Other animals eat the part of the plant that holds the water and try to avoid getting pricked by the spines.

Meat-eating plants

Some plants do not get all the nutrients they need from the soil, so they **consume**, or eat, insects! More than 400 types of plants are meat-eaters. These plants make their own food using the sun's energy, but insects give them the extra nutrients they need to help them grow bigger and healthier.

A pitcher plant has slippery leaves. Insects slip down a leaf and drown in liquid at the bottom. Hairs that point downward stop the insects from crawling out. The plant uses special juices to break down the insects.

Herbivores

Herbivores, or animals that eat mainly plants, are at the second level of all food chains. They are also called **primary consumers**. Consumers are animals that consume other living things. Primary consumers are the "first" consumers in a food chain. Herbivores include small squirrels that eat nuts and berries and huge elephants that eat grass and tree bark.

Herbivores have a hard time getting energy out of plants because grass, buds, leaves, and twigs are difficult for their body to **digest**, or break down. Most herbivores have to eat a lot of plants to get the energy they need. Elephants and cows must spend most of their time eating in order to get enough nutrients and energy to stay healthy. Many grass-eating animals have ridges on their teeth for grinding their food into small pieces so their body can digest it more easily.

*Many birds are herbivores. Some, such as this budgerigar, eat mainly seeds. Others, including parrots, eat fruits and nuts. A few, such as sunbirds and hummingbirds, feed on the **nectar**, or sweet juices, inside flowers.*

Herbivores often have special body parts for getting the food they need. Giraffes have a long neck to reach the green leaves on the tops of tall acacia trees.

Chewing cud

Some herbivores have to re-chew their food in order to break it down enough for their body to absorb its energy. The food comes back up into their mouth after it has been in their stomach for a while. They chew this food, called **cud**, again before swallowing it a second time. Sheep, cows, and deer are examples of animals that chew their food twice.

Some herbivores eat an entire plant. Others eat certain parts, such as seeds, fruits, or flowers. Many caterpillars eat only the leaves of plants.

Carnivores

Carnivores are animals that eat mainly other animals. Most carnivores feed on herbivores, so they are called **secondary consumers**. A few carnivores eat other carnivores. They are called **tertiary consumers**. Some carnivores can be both secondary and tertiary consumers. For example, in the food web on pages 22-23, a lynx is a secondary consumer when it eats a rabbit, which is a herbivore. When a lynx eats a weasel, another carnivore, the lynx is a tertiary consumer.

*A **species**, or type, of animal that is eaten by nothing else in the food web is called a **top predator**. For example, large sharks are the top predators of several food chains because no animals prey on them.*

Predators and prey

Most carnivores are **predators**. A predator is an animal that hunts and kills other animals for food. The animal that a predator eats is called **prey**. A huge variety of animals are predators, from spiders that eat flies to lions that hunt zebras. Predators are very important in an ecosystem. Without them, the number of herbivores would increase until there were no longer enough plants to eat. Predators often eat only sick and weak animals, leaving more food for healthy animals and their babies.

A praying mantis is an insect that kills other insects, such as flies, for food.

Meat-eating plants such as this pitcher plant cannot move to find prey. They wait for an insect to fly or crawl onto them.

*Ospreys are **raptors**, or birds of prey. They have strong, hooked beaks and curved claws called **talons** for catching prey and tearing flesh.*

Hunting and scavenging

Each type of predator has a different way of catching food. Some, such as wolves, track their prey over long distances. A few, including lions and leopards, **stalk**, or sneak close to, their prey and then chase and catch it. Other predators wait quietly while watching for any movement nearby. When prey comes close, they grab it. Frogs and some birds hunt this way.

(left) Bee-eaters do not consume just bees. They eat all types of flying insects. They catch their prey in midair.

(right) Some predators set a trap for their prey. Many spiders build a sticky web and wait for a meal to fly or crawl into it.

Scavengers

A type of carnivore that feeds mainly on dead animals that it finds is called a scavenger. Scavengers such as vultures help keep an ecosystem clean. They often eat the leftovers from a predator's meal. Scavengers are an important part of a food web because they keep the food energy in a dead animal's body from being wasted.

(right) On the African savannah, wild dogs sometimes hunt together in packs, but they also scavenge.

(below) Vultures wait patiently for a nearby predator to finish eating before they rush in to feast on the leftovers.

Omnivores

Omnivores are animals that eat both plants and animals. In most types of ecosystems, omnivores do not have difficulty finding food because they eat almost anything they find. An omnivore can belong to several levels of a food web at once, depending on what type of food it eats. Bears, pigs, raccoons, and humans are some examples of omnivores.

Grizzlies make a meal out of almost anything. They eat roots, berries, fish, insects, birds, other animals, and **carrion***, or dead animal flesh. This mother and cub are enjoying a lunch of fresh, green grass.*

Opportunistic feeders

Most omnivores are **opportunistic feeders**, which means they eat whatever is available. Their **diet**, or the type of foods they eat, changes depending on the time of year. Bears, for example, often eat fish in the spring and berries in the fall. An omnivore's diet also changes depending on whatever it finds nearby. Ostriches usually eat grass, but they readily eat any lizards they find crawling in the grass.

(top) Raccoons eat mice, frogs, shellfish, crabs, worms, insects, fruit, vegetables, and garbage!

(above) Some bird omnivores eat insects at one time of the year and seeds at other times.

(left) Humans eat many types of food, from fruits and vegetables to chicken and fish.

Decomposers

All living things die. If herbivores or carnivores do not eat them immediately, the bodies of dead plants and animals are usually broken down by **decomposers**. Decomposers are living things that get all their food energy from dead material. They form the **detritus food web**. Detritus means garbage. Bacteria, worms, slugs, snails, and fungi such as mushrooms, are examples of decomposers.

The greatest recyclers

Decomposers recycle important nutrients and help keep them moving through food webs. Without fungi and other decomposers, nutrients would stay locked up in dead animals, branches, logs, and leaves. They could not be used by plants to grow. If plants could not grow, they would not survive. Without plants, all other living things would slowly starve.

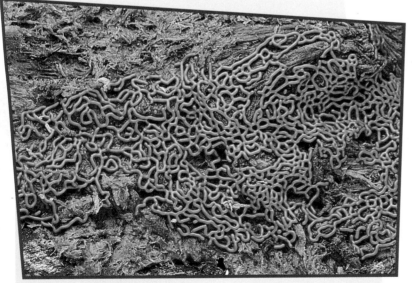

On the forest floor, slime molds such as this pretzel slime mold spread over dead logs and slowly break them down.

Breaking down their food

Decomposers are very small, so many kinds are needed to help break down large pieces of dead material. On land, animals such as snails, mites, and earthworms eat parts of dead plants, herbivores, and carnivores in order to start the breakdown process. In water, small **crustaceans** such as crabs and insect **larvae**, or babies, are an important part of the detritus food web.

An earthworm consumes dead leaves and other detritus on the ground.

Nature's clean-up crew

Decomposers get the energy they need from dead material, but they also help keep the ecosystem clean for other living things. Without decomposers to feed on dead material, an ecosystem such as a forest would soon be buried under piles of dead plants and animals.

Snails are an important part of the detritus food web because their favorite food is dead leaves. Snails chew up the leaves and leave small pieces that are easier for fungi and bacteria to break down.

A forest food web

Food chains and webs are different in each ecosystem. For example, the food web in a forest ecosystem has many plants and animals that only live in forests. Many food chains and webs also change with the seasons of the year. A summer food web in a forest has many more members than a winter one because some animals migrate or sleep. One part of the summer food web is shown on these two pages. The arrowheads point toward the living things that receive the food energy.

crossbill (o)

ants (o)

mouse (o)

(below) Sometimes a regular food web and a detritus food web connect because some larger animals eat decomposers. Badgers, for example, eat earthworms as part of their diet.

The many food chains in this forest make up the forest food web.

badger (c)

weasel (c)

earthworms & beetles (d)

mushrooms & other fungi (d)

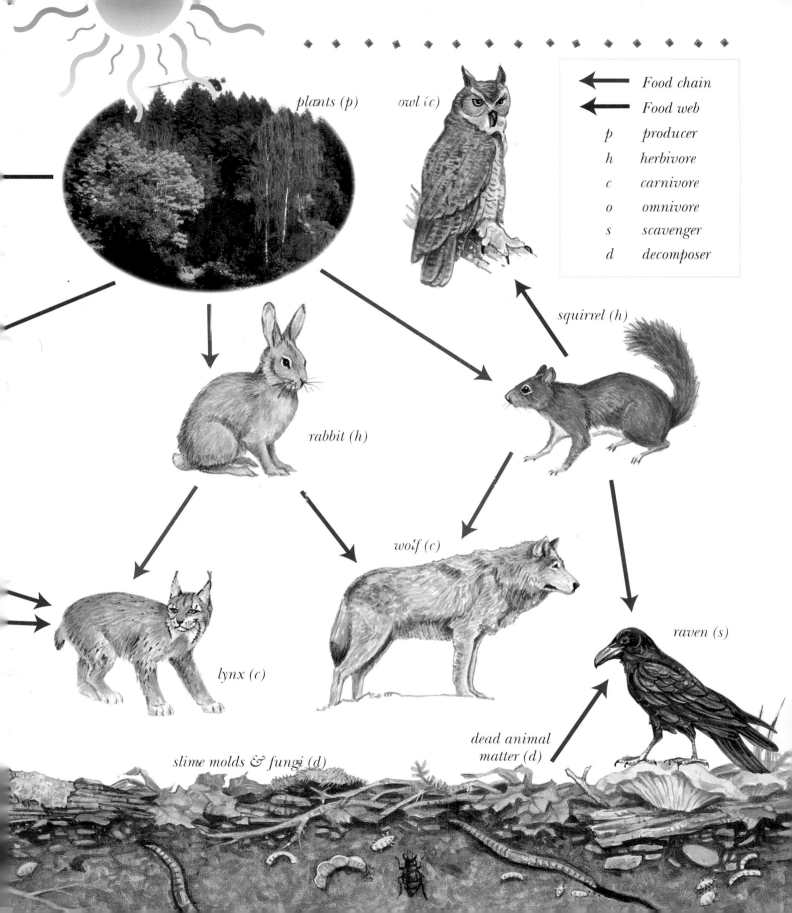

plants (p)

owl (c)

squirrel (h)

rabbit (h)

wolf (c)

lynx (c)

raven (s)

dead animal matter (d)

slime molds & fungi (d)

Food chain
Food web
p   producer
h   herbivore
c   carnivore
o   omnivore
s   scavenger
d   decomposer

A web on the reef

Coral reefs grow in warm, clear, shallow salt water. They are made by thousands of little animals called **polyps**. So many types of creatures live in coral reefs that scientists have not yet counted all of them! Coral reef food chains and webs have many members and many connections, but a simple example is pictured on these pages.

What eats what?

Phytoplankton are the primary producers of the coral reef food web. Tiny animals called **zooplankton** are primary consumers because they eat phytoplankton. The name "zooplankton" means "wandering animals." Zooplankton include newly hatched shrimp, crabs, fish, and sea worms. Coral polyps eat zooplankton, so they are at the third level of the coral reef food web.

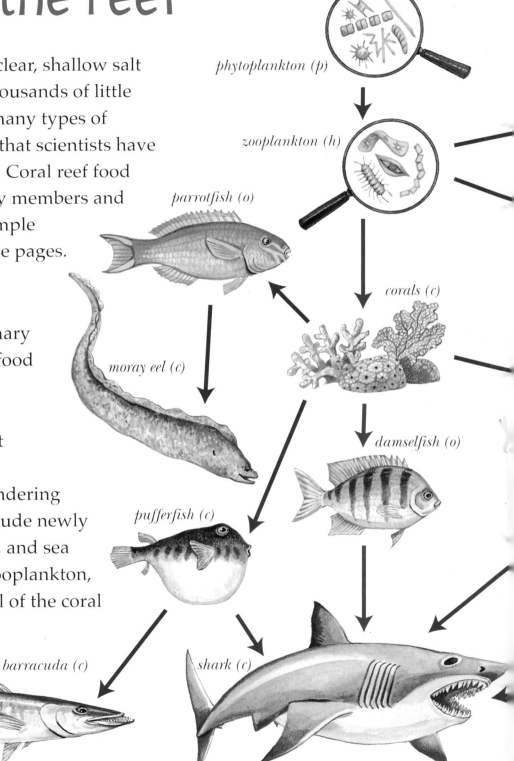

phytoplankton (p)

zooplankton (h)

parrotfish (o)

corals (c)

moray eel (c)

damselfish (o)

pufferfish (c)

barracuda (c)

shark (c)

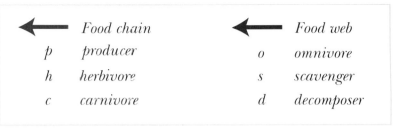

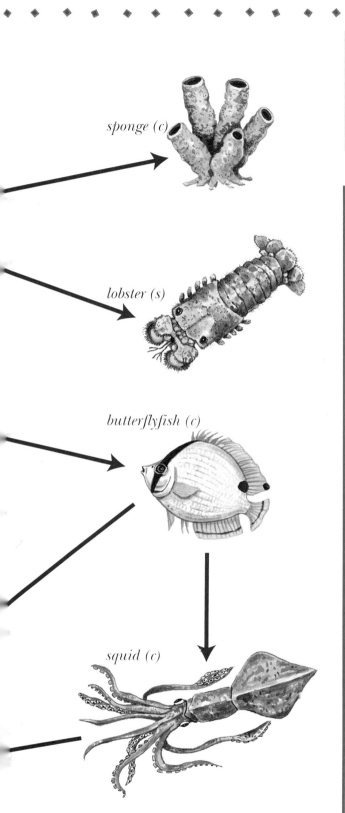

sponge (c)

lobster (s)

butterflyfish (c)

squid (c)

Finding food as a janitor

Some ocean animals find their food on the body of another animal. They are called **cleaners** because they help other animals stay clean and healthy. About 50 fish species and a few types of shrimp are cleaners. They eat food pieces, algae, and **parasites** off the body of larger fish. Parasites are tiny animals that get their nourishment from the body of another, larger animal, called a **host**. Parasites often make their host sick. The large fish do not eat the cleaners that help them get rid of parasites. Some even let a cleaner go right inside their mouth!

Arctic food web

snowy owl (c)

raven (s)

caribou (h)

arctic wolf (c)

arctic hare (h)

ptarmigan (h)

arctic fox (c)

musk ox (h)

plants (p)

lemming (h)

The Arctic is an area of land and water at the far north of the earth. For most of the year, the Arctic Ocean is completely covered by a huge sheet of ice. The land is called **tundra**. The arctic tundra is a treeless ecosystem that has long, harsh winters and short, cool summers. The ground beneath the tundra surface, called **permafrost**, stays frozen all year round.

In the summer, many animals find enough food on the tundra. Mosses and small shrubs provide food for several species of herbivores. Visiting birds eat insects such as mosquitoes. Other carnivores, such as wolves and owls, feed on the birds and the herbivores. In the winter, most of the birds and many of the herbivores leave the tundra to find food in warmer areas to the south.

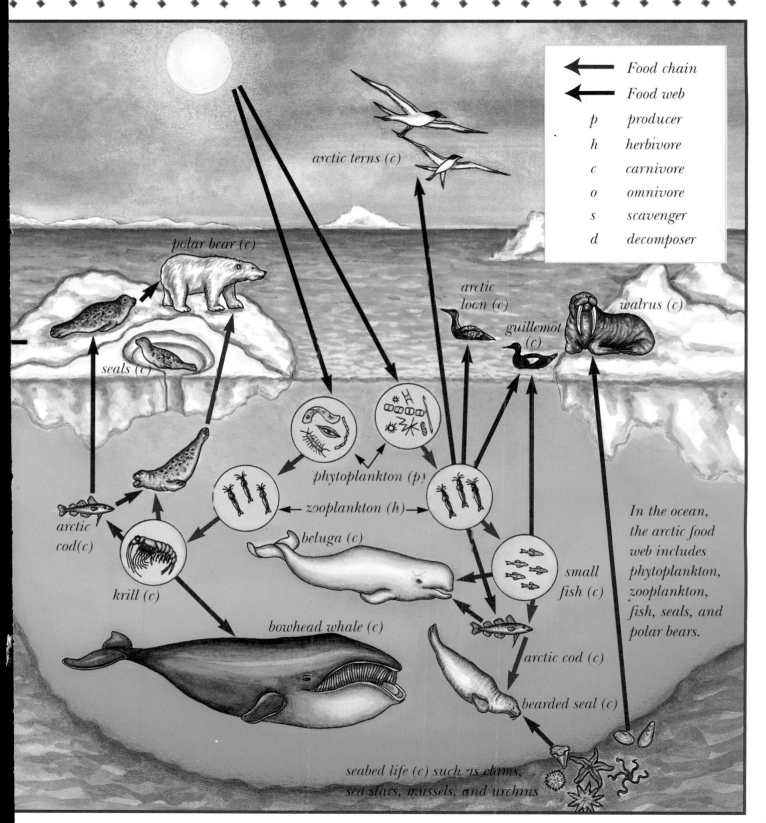

polar bear (c)

arctic terns (c)

Food chain
Food web
p — producer
h — herbivore
c — carnivore
o — omnivore
s — scavenger
d — decomposer

seals (c)

arctic loon (c)

guillemot (c)

walrus (c)

phytoplankton (p)

zooplankton (h)

beluga (c)

arctic cod (c)

krill (c)

small fish (c)

bowhead whale (c)

arctic cod (c)

In the ocean, the arctic food web includes phytoplankton, zooplankton, fish, seals, and polar bears.

bearded seal (c)

seabed life (c) such as clams, sea stars, mussels, and urchins

A savannah food web

Many different grasses thrive on the African savannah. Grass-eating zebras, gazelles, antelopes, and wildebeests find plenty of food there. Other herbivores such as giraffes feed on the few acacia trees that grow in the grassland.

The savannah has a wet season and a dry season. During the wet season in a certain area, herbivores gather to feed on the new grass that grows. When the rains stop and the grasses begin to die, most herbivores travel to wetter areas in search of fresh food.

Ostriches are omnivores that eat a lot of grass, as well as anything nearby, such as fruit, seeds, insects, and small animals.

A smorgasbord for predators

Many herbivores feed on the grasslands, so it is also a good place for carnivores to find a meal. Predators in the savannah include cheetahs, hyenas, leopards, and lions. Scavengers also find a lot of food. Marabou storks, vultures, jackals, and sometimes hyenas clean up after the carnivores.

Scavengers such as vultures look for carnivores that are hunting. When an animal is killed, vultures also get a meal.

Zebras on the savannah are primary consumers. They eat mainly grass and sometimes the shoots and leaves of bushes.

Lions and other carnivores, such as cheetahs and leopards, are the secondary consumers on the savannah.

Food web game

With a group of eight to ten friends and a ball of string, you can find out how all living things are connected through food chains and webs. One person, who holds the ball of string, pretends to be the sun. One person pretends to be many kinds of plants, and other friends pretend to be herbivores and carnivores.

To play the food web game, the sun holds onto the end of the string and passes the ball to the person pretending to be many plants. He or she holds onto some string and passes the ball to a herbivore, and then to a carnivore to form a food chain. Other animals hold onto the string at different places to form a food web, as shown below.

plants *herbivore* *carnivore* *sun* *carnivore* *carnivore* *herbivore* *decomposer*

If a carnivore or herbivore becomes extinct, then one person drops out of the game and the string sags to show that the food web has been disrupted.

Words to know

absorb To take in

carbon dioxide A colorless, odorless gas that is part of air

carnivore An animal that eats mainly meat

chlorophyll A green substance that is used during photosynthesis and is found in the leaves of plants

consume To eat

consumer A living thing that must eat other living things for food and energy

decomposer A living thing that breaks down dead plant and animal material in order to get food energy

detritus food web A food web made up of decomposers and other animals that feed on dead plant and animal material

ecosystem A certain area that includes all the plants, animals, and non-living natural things, such as sand, rocks, and soil

energy The power needed to do things

food chain A pattern of eating and being eaten; for example, a plant is eaten by a rabbit, which is then eaten by a fox

food web Two or more food chains that connect when a member of one food chain eats a member of another food chain

herbivore An animal that eats mainly plants

larva A baby insect just after it hatches from an egg

microscope An instrument scientists look through to make tiny things appear larger

nutrient A substance that living things get from food, which is needed for growth and good health

omnivore An animal that eats both plants and animals

oxygen A colorless, odorless gas that is part of air and which humans, animals, and plants need to breathe in order to survive

photosynthesis The process that plants use to trap the sun's energy and store it in the form of food

phytoplankton Tiny plants that live in water

predator An animal that hunts and kills other animals for food

prey An animal that is eaten by predators

producer A green plant, which is the first food maker in a food chain

savannah A broad, grassy plain that is often treeless and is located in tropical areas

scavenger An animal that eats dead animal flesh

top predator The predator at the top of a food chain

tertiary Describing something that is third in order or place

zooplankton Tiny animals that live in water and feed on phytoplankton

Index

4 5 6 7 8 9 0   Printed in the U.S.A.   7 6 5 4 3 2 1 0